# Pokémon

# FIRE

# POKÉDEX

BY KATHERINE NOLL AND TRACEY WEST

**SCHOLASTIC INC.**

New York   Toronto   London   Auckland   Sydney
Mexico City   New Delhi   Hong Kong   Buenos Aires

# You're on Your Way!

Welcome! There are many different Types of Pokémon. This book is about a very hot Type— the Fire Type Pokémon. Here, you will find:

* Stats for 28 Fire Pokémon.
* Tips for using Fire Pokémon in battle.
* The best places to battle with Fire Pokémon.
* The story of an exciting Fire Pokémon battle!
* A talk with Professor Birch.
* Cool info about Pokémon Centers.

When you are done with this book, you should be a Fire Pokémon Master! So start reading! The world of Fire Pokémon is waiting for you.

# About Fire Pokémon

You go to a Pokémon Gym to see a battle. As you get near, you see flames burst from the Gym! Is it a fire? No—it's a Fire Pokémon battle. Fire Pokémon are a good choice for a Trainer who battles a lot. That's because Fire attacks pack a lot of power. A move like Smokescreen can cause another Pokémon's move to miss your Pokémon. The Ember attack sends hot sparks flying in the air.

Of course, most Fire Pokémon are famous for their flame attacks. Flamethrower, Fire Spin, and Flame Wheel all send flames blazing across the field.

Different Fire Pokémon have different ways of using Fire attacks. Some shoot flames from their mouth. Others can shoot fire out of their head, back, or tail.

Fire Pokémon can be a good choice for new Trainers. In the Kanto region, a Trainer can choose **Charmander** as a starter Pokémon. But a **Charmander** can be hard to train. Just ask Pokémon Trainer Ash Ketchum.

Ash's **Charmander** evolved before Ash was ready. When it became a **Charizard**, it never wanted to do anything Ash asked. Ash lost some battles because of his **Charizard**.

So if you choose or capture a Fire Pokémon, train it well. It may give you a hard time at first. But with practice, your Fire Pokémon could blaze the way to victory!

# Battle Tips
# for Fire Types

A Pokémon Trainer needs to know which Type of Pokémon to choose in a battle. Some Types have an advantage over other Types. (It's a bit like the game Rock-Paper-Scissors.)
If you battle with Fire Type Pokémon, this chart can help.

## Fire Types Are Good Against:

✳ Grass Types such as **Treecko**. Fire burns grass.
✳ Ice Types such as **Snorunt**. Fire melts ice.
✳ Bug Types such as **Ledyba** and **Wurmple**.
✳ Steel Types such as **Steelix**. Hot flames can melt metal.

## Fire Types Are Bad Against:

✳ Water Types such as **Mudkip**. Water puts out fire, of course!

✳ Ground Types such as **Sandslash**. It's not easy to burn dirt!

✳ Rock Types such as **Geodude**. It's pretty hard to melt a rock!

When it comes to Fire Types, these Pokémon can't be beat. **Charmander** has lots of attack power. When **Charmander** evolves into **Charmeleon**, the flame on the tip of its tail becomes very strong. And when **Charmeleon** evolves into **Charizard**, look out! This Pokémon has superhot attacks!

## Charmander
Lizard Pokémon

**Pronunciation:**
CHAR-man-der

**Possible Moves:**
Scratch, Growl, Ember, Leer, Rage, Slash, Flamethrower, Fire Spin, Smokescreen, Scary Face, Dragon Rage, Metal Claw

**Evolves:** at level 16

## Charmeleon
Flame Pokémon

**Pronunciation:**
char-MEAL-ee-ehn

**Possible Moves:**
Scratch, Growl, Ember, Leer, Rage, Slash, Flamethrower, Fire Spin, Smokescreen, Scary Face, Dragon Rage, Metal Claw

**Evolves:** at level 36

## Charizard
Flame Pokémon

**Pronunciation:**
CHAR-i-zard

**Possible Moves:**
Scratch, Growl, Ember, Slash, Flamethrower, Fire Spin, Smokescreen, Scary Face, Dragon Rage, Wing Attack, Heat Wave, Metal Claw

**Does not evolve**

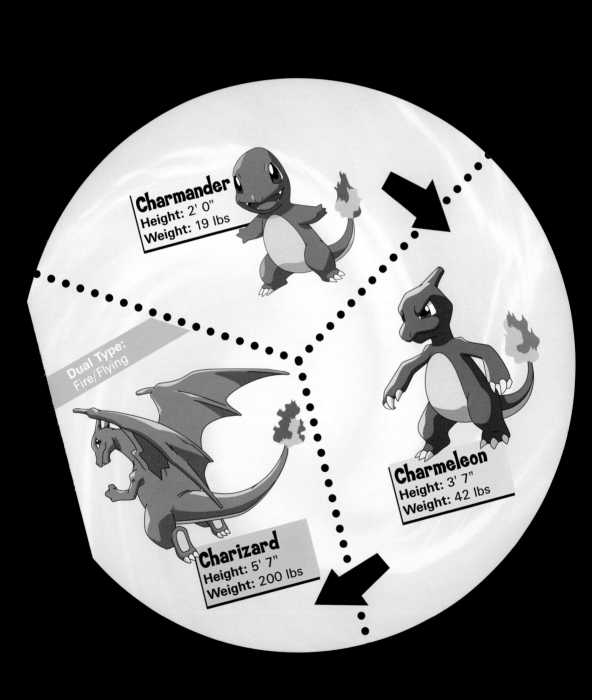

**Charmander**
Height: 2' 0"
Weight: 19 lbs

**Charmeleon**
Height: 3' 7"
Weight: 42 lbs

**Charizard**
Height: 5' 7"
Weight: 200 lbs

Dual Type:
Fire/Flying

**Growlithe** has a super sense of smell. Once it smells anything, this Pokémon won't forget the scent—no matter what! It can also use its sense of smell to determine the feelings of other living things. So it's no surprise that **Arcanine**, the evolved form of **Growlithe**, helps Officer Jenny fight crime in the Pokémon world.

## Growlithe
**Puppy Pokémon**

**Pronunciation:**
GROWL-ith

**Possible Moves:** Bite, Roar, Ember, Leer, Take Down, Agility, Flamethrower, Odor Sleuth, Flame Wheel, Helping Hand

**Evolves:** with a Fire Stone

## Arcanine
**Legendary Pokémon**

**Pronunciation:**
ar-kuh-NINE

**Possible Moves:** Roar, Bite, Ember, Odor Sleuth, Extreme Speed

**Does not evolve**

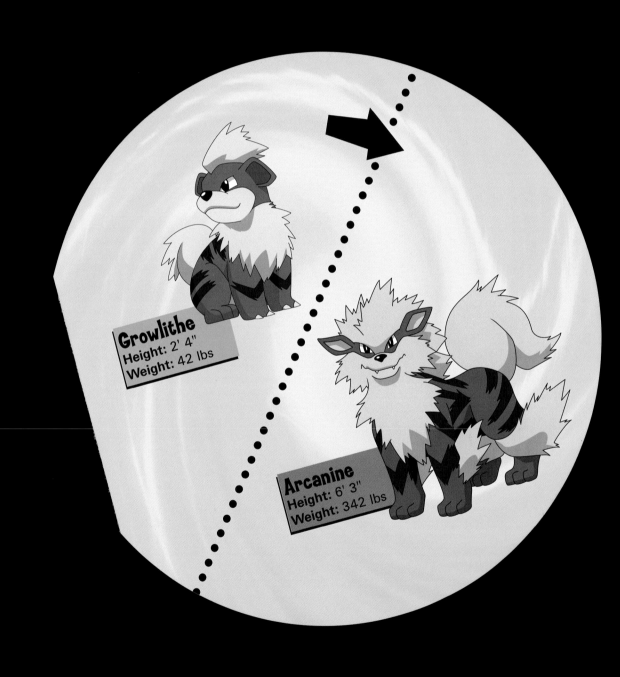

**Growlithe**
Height: 2' 4"
Weight: 42 lbs

**Arcanine**
Height: 6' 3"
Weight: 342 lbs

If you like Pokémon that are hot and fast, then these two are for you! At birth a **Ponyta** is weak. But as it tries to keep up with its parents, it becomes stonger and faster! And **Rapidash** uses its super speed when it attacks. But if you want to catch **Ponyta** or **Rapidash**, you have to be quick! They might race away before you can even throw your Poké Ball.

## Ponyta
**Fire Horse Pokémon**

**Pronunciation:**
po-NEE-tuh

**Possible Moves:**
Ember, Tail Whip, Stomp, Growl, Fire Spin, Take Down, Agility, Quick Attack, Bounce, Fire Blast

**Evolves:** at level 40

## Rapidash
**Fire Horse Pokémon**

**Pronunciation:**
RAP-i-dash

**Possible Moves:**
Ember, Tail Whip, Stomp, Growl, Fire Spin, Take Down, Agility, Quick Attack, Fury Attack, Bounce, Fire Blast

**Does not evolve**

**Ponyta**
Height: 3' 3"
Weight: 66 lbs

**Rapidash**
Height: 5' 7"
Weight: 209 lbs

Which came first, **Magby** or **Magmar**? Well, that depends. If you capture a **Magby**, you can train it until it evolves into a **Magmar**. But if you capture a **Magmar**, you can breed it with another **Magmar** to get a **Magby**. Then you have a baby Pokémon to care for! It's easy to tell if your **Magby** is healthy. When it feels good, yellow flames burst from its mouth. When it is tired, black smoke is mixed in with the yellow flames.

## Magby
### Live Coal Pokémon

**Pronunciation:**
MAG-bee

**Possible Moves:**
Ember, Smog, Fire Punch, Smokescreen, Sunny Day, Leer, Flamethrower, Confuse Ray, Fire Blast

**Evolves:** at level 30

## Magmar
### Spitfire Pokémon

**Pronunciation:**
MAG-mar

**Possible Moves:**
Ember, Leer, Confuse Ray, Fire Punch, Smokescreen, Smog, Flamethrower, Sunny Day, Fire Blast

**Does not evolve**

**Magby**
Height: 2' 4"
Weight: 47 lbs

**Magmar**
Height: 4' 3"
Weight: 98 lbs

**Tip:**
You can breed many kinds of Pokémon together to get a new young Pokémon. For example, you could breed a male and female **Jigglypuff** to get an **Igglybuff**. Just take them to the nearest Pokémon Breeding center. The female will lay an egg, and before you know it, you'll have a brand-new Pokémon.

Many Pokémon evolve after they gain levels. But some Pokémon can only evolve with the use of special stones.

The Pokémon **Eevee** has more evolutions than any other Pokémon. If you use a Fire Stone on your **Eevee**, it will evolve into **Flareon**, a Fire Pokémon. This Pokémon stores energy from the Sun in its body. That makes its body get hotter than 1,600 degrees Fahrenheit. **Flareon** is one hot Pokémon!

## Flareon
**Flame Pokémon**

**Pronunciation:**
FLARE-ee-on

**Possible Moves:** Tackle, Sand-Attack, Quick Attack, Ember, Tail Whip, Bite, Leer, Fire Spin, Smog, Flamethrower

**Does not evolve**

16

**Eevee**
**(Normal Type)**

**Flareon**
Height: 2' 11"
Weight: 55 lbs

If you are ever traveling through the Orange Islands, be on the lookout for **Moltres**. Should you see this Legendary Pokémon fly through the air, you are lucky. It is a beautiful sight. Red flames leap from its head. It looks like its wings and tail are made of flames. But you won't see **Moltres** for long. If spotted, **Moltres** disappears in a flash of fire.

## Moltres
**Flame Pokémon**

**Pronunciation:**
MOLE-trace

**Possible Moves:** Fire Spin, Leer, Agility, Sky Attack, Wing Attack, Ember, Endure, Flamethrower, Safeguard, Heat Wave

**Does not evolve**

**Dual Type:** Fire/Flying

**Moltres**
Height: 6' 7"
Weight: 132 lbs

19

**Cyndaquil** seems shy, but watch out! It can shoot flames out of its back! **Quilava**, Cyndaquil's evolved form, can dodge attacks while scorching its foe with strong flames. And **Typhlosion**, the final evolution, is big, bad, and boiling! It can cause huge explosions by rubbing together the fur on its back.

## Cyndaquil
**Fire Mouse Pokémon**

**Pronunciation:**
SIN-da-kwil

**Possible Moves:**
Tackle, Leer, Smokescreen, Ember, Quick Attack, Flame Wheel, Swift, Flamethrower

**Evolves:** at level 14

## Quilava
**Volcano Pokémon**

**Pronunciation:**
Kwi-LA-va

**Possible Moves:**
Tackle, Leer, Smokescreen, Ember Quick Attack, Flame Wheel, Swift, Flamethrower

**Evolves:** at level 36

## Typhlosion
**Volcano Pokémon**

**Pronunciation:**
tie-FLOW-shun

**Possible Moves:**
Tackle, Leer, Smokescreen, Ember, Quick Attack, Flame Wheel, Swift, Flamethrower

**Does not evolve**

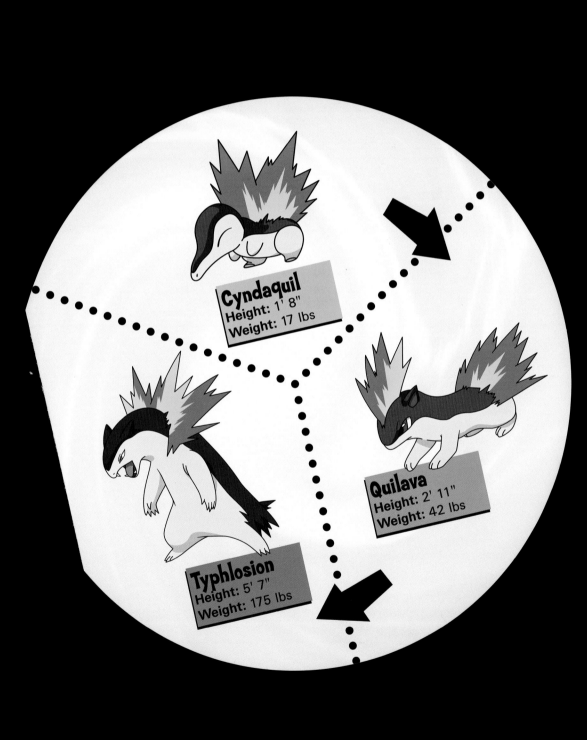

**Cyndaquil**
Height: 1' 8"
Weight: 17 lbs

**Quilava**
Height: 2' 11"
Weight: 42 lbs

**Typhlosion**
Height: 5' 7"
Weight: 175 lbs

A **Vulpix** is born with only one white tail. If its Trainer loves it and cares for it, **Vulpix**'s tail will change color and split into six separate tails. The lovely **Vulpix** can evolve into the beautiful **Ninetales**. There are many rumors about the magical powers of its tails. One legend says **Ninetales** can live over 1,000 years thanks to its special tails! We might never know all its secrets.

## Vulpix
**Fox Pokémon**

**Pronunciation:**
VUHL-picks

**Possible Moves:**
Ember, Tail Whip, Quick Attack, Confuse Ray, Safeguard, Roar, Flamethrower, Fire Spin, Will-O-Wisp, Imprison, Grudge

**Evolves:** with a Fire Stone

## Ninetales
**Fox Pokémon**

**Pronunciation:**
NINE-tails

**Possible Moves:** Fire Spin, Quick Attack, Confuse Ray, Ember, Safeguard

**Does not evolve**

**Vulpix**
Height: 2' 0"
Weight: 22 lbs

**Ninetales**
Height: 3' 7"
Weight: 44 lbs

The Legendary **Entei** is very mysterious. It is said that **Entei** was born from the eruption of a volcano, which gave the Pokémon great power. **Entei's** massive bursts of flame can burn up all that they touch. This great power makes it almost impossible for anyone to catch **Entei**. In addition, **Entei** will usually run away rather than battle a Trainer. Ash once met a Trainer who was sure his **Misdreavus**—and its move called Mean Look—would be enough to keep **Entei** in one place long enough to capture it. But the Legendary Pokémon was able to escape and continue to run free.

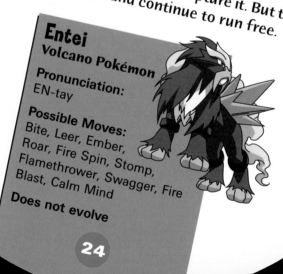

## Entei
**Volcano Pokémon**

**Pronunciation:**
EN-tay

**Possible Moves:**
Bite, Leer, Ember, Roar, Fire Spin, Stomp, Flamethrower, Swagger, Fire Blast, Calm Mind

**Does not evolve**

24

**Entei**
Height: 6' 11"
Weight: 437 lbs

25

This colorful Legendary Pokémon loves to fly. Its body and wings glow with all of the colors of the rainbow. In fact, **Ho-Oh** is said to live at the bottom of a rainbow.

When Ash first started his journey, he spotted **Ho-Oh** flying high in the sky. Will he ever come face-to-face with this Legendary bird?

# Ho-Oh
**Rainbow Pokémon**

**Pronunciation:**
HO-oh

**Possible Moves:** Sacred Fire, Safeguard, Gust, Recover, Fire Blast, Sunny Day, Swift, Whirlwind, Ancientpower, Future Sight

**Does not evolve**

26

**Dual Type:** Fire/Flying

**Ho-Oh**
Height: 12' 6"
Weight: 439 lbs

27

**Torchic** is so cute! But it packs a lot of fire power. It can breathe flames that reach 1,800 degrees Fahrenheit! **Combusken**, **Torchic's** evolved form, has Fighting abilities as well as Fire attacks. And **Blaziken**, the final evolution, is really fierce. Once, Ash battled his **Charizard** against another Trainer's **Blaziken**. It was an amazing battle, but **Blaziken** won in the end.

## Torchic
**Chick Pokémon**

**Pronunciation:**
TORE-chick

**Possible Moves:**
Scratch, Growl, Focus Energy, Ember, Peck, Sand-Attack, Fire Spin, Quick Attack, Slash, Mirror Move, Flamethrower

**Evolves:** at level 16

## Combusken
**Young Fowl Pokémon**

**Pronunciation:**
kom-BUSK-in

**Possible Moves:**
Scratch, Growl, Focus Energy, Ember, Double Kick, Peck, Sand-Attack, Slash, Mirror Move, Sky Uppercut, Quick Attack, Bulk Up

**Evolves:** at level 36

## Blaziken
**Blaze Pokémon**

**Pronunciation:**
BLAZE-uh-kin

**Possible Moves:** Fire Punch, Scratch, Growl, Focus Energy, Ember, Double Kick, Peck, Sand-Attack, Bulk Up, Quick Attack, Blaze Kick, Slash, Mirror Move, Sky Uppercut

**Does not evolve**

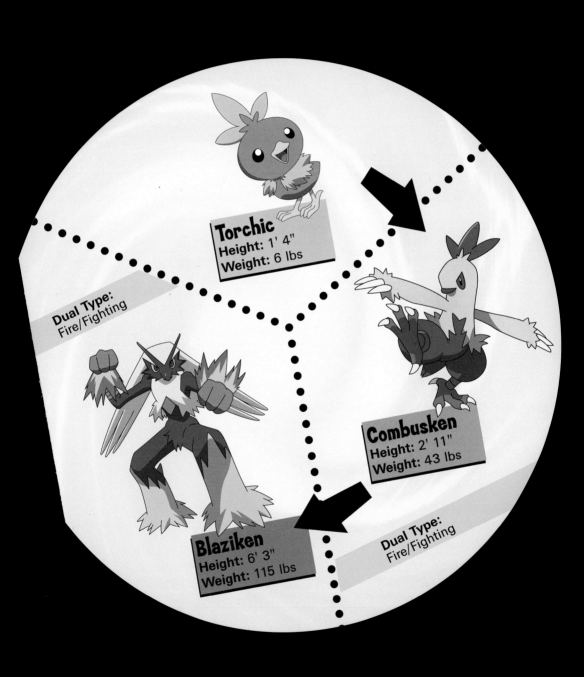

**Torchic**
Height: 1' 4"
Weight: 6 lbs

**Combusken**
Height: 2' 11"
Weight: 43 lbs

**Blaziken**
Height: 6' 3"
Weight: 115 lbs

Dual Type:
Fire/Fighting

Dual Type:
Fire/Fighting

**Numel** and **Camerupt** may not be the smartest or fastest Pokémon around. But they both pack enough fire power to make up for it. **Numel's** body stores boiling hot magma that reaches 2,200 degrees Fahrenheit. And **Camerupt** has an actual volcano inside its body. Sometimes superhot lava will shoot out of the humps on its back!

## Numel
**Numb Pokémon**

**Pronunciation:**
NOOM-uhl

**Possible Moves:**
Growl, Tackle, Ember, Magnitude, Focus Energy, Take Down, Amnesia, Earthquake, Flamethrower, Double-Edge

**Evolves:** at level 33

## Camerupt
**Eruption Pokémon**

**Pronunciation:**
CAM-uhr-upt

**Possible Moves:**
Growl, Tackle, Ember, Magnitude, Focus Energy, Take Down, Amnesia, Rock Slide, Earthquake, Eruption, Fissure

**Does not evolve**

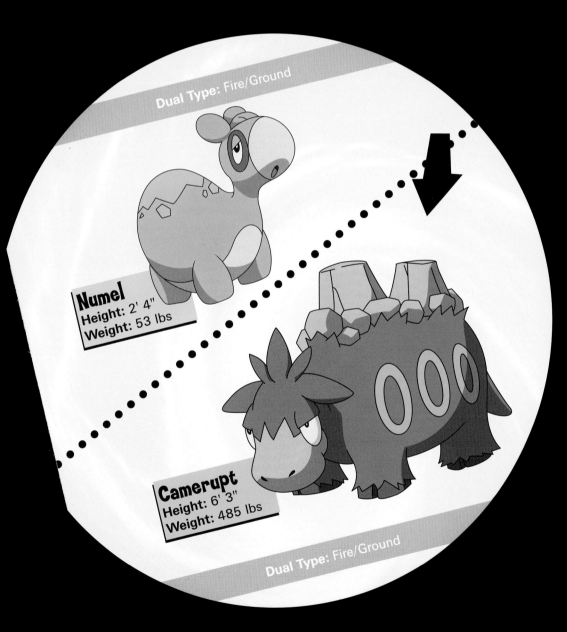

Dual Type: Fire/Ground

**Numel**
Height: 2' 4"
Weight: 53 lbs

**Camerupt**
Height: 6' 3"
Weight: 485 lbs

Dual Type: Fire/Ground

If you ever visit a volcano, you might see some **Slugma** crawling around. **Slugma** never sleep! Their bodies are filled with magma. If they slow down, the magma will cool and harden.

And hot magma cooling into rock is what makes **Magcargo**, **Slugma's** evolved form, both a Fire and a Rock Type Pokémon. **Magcargo's** shell is really made of hot magma that has cooled. It may look as hard as a rock, but **Magcargo's** shell is very fragile and will crumble at the slightest touch.

## Slugma
**Lava Pokémon**

**Pronunciation:**
SLUG-muh

**Possible Moves:**
Smog, Ember, Rock Throw, Harden, Amnesia, Yawn, Flamethrower, Rock Slide, Body Slam

**Evolves:** at level 38

## Magcargo
**Lava Pokémon**

**Pronunciation:**
mag-CAR-go

**Possible Moves:**
Smog, Ember, Rock Throw, Harden, Amnesia, Yawn, Flamethrower, Rock Slide, Body Slam

**Does not evolve**

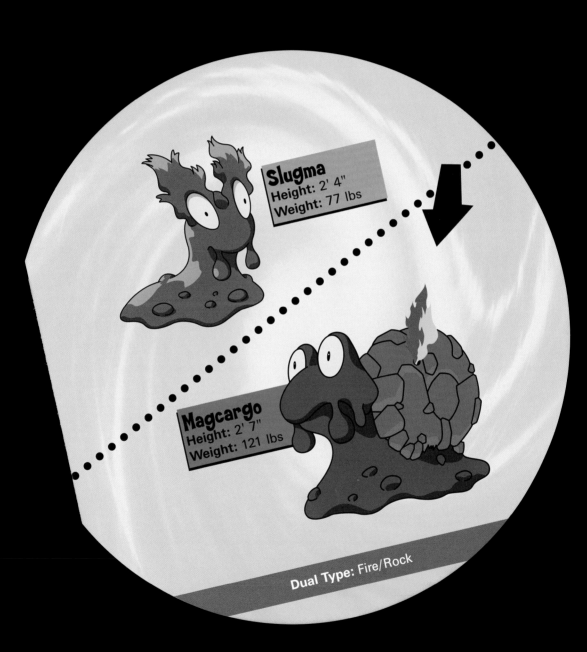

**Slugma**
Height: 2' 4"
Weight: 77 lbs

**Magcargo**
Height: 2' 7"
Weight: 121 lbs

Dual Type: Fire/Rock

Both **Houndour** and **Houndoom** are a combination of Dark and Fire Types. If you hear strange howls or cries in the forest, it could be a pack of **Houndour**, trying to locate prey.

Maybe you'll hear the eerie howls of **Houndoom** as you walk through a forest at night. If you're not trying to catch one, you might want to run the other way.

## Houndour
**Dark Pokémon**

**Pronunciation:**
hown-DOUR

**Attacks:** Leer, Ember, Roar, Smog, Bite, Faint Attack, Flamethrower, Crunch, Howl, Odor Sleuth

**Evolves:** at level 24

## Houndoom
**Dark Pokémon**

**Pronunciation:**
hown-DOOM

**Possible Moves:** Faint Attack, Flamethrower, Bite, Leer, Ember, Roar, Smog, Crunch, Howl

**Does not evolve**

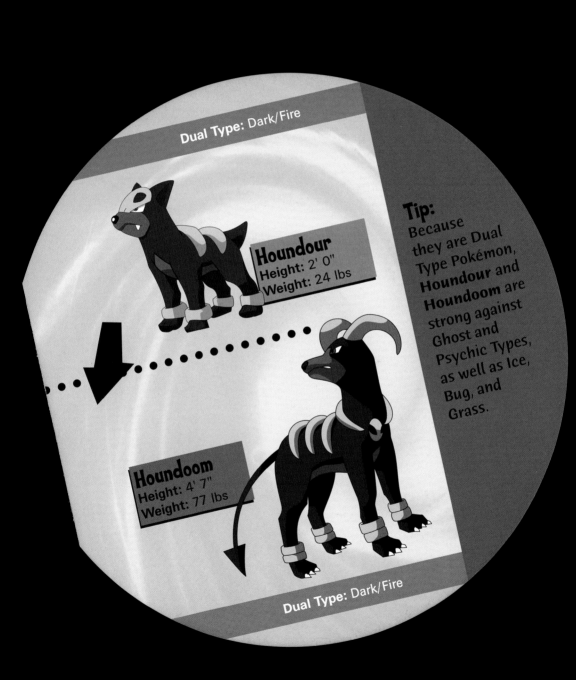

Dual Type: Dark/Fire

**Houndour**
Height: 2' 0"
Weight: 24 lbs

**Tip:**
Because they are Dual Type Pokémon, **Houndour** and **Houndoom** are strong against Ghost and Psychic Types, as well as Ice, Bug, and Grass.

**Houndoom**
Height: 4' 7"
Weight: 77 lbs

Dual Type: Dark/Fire

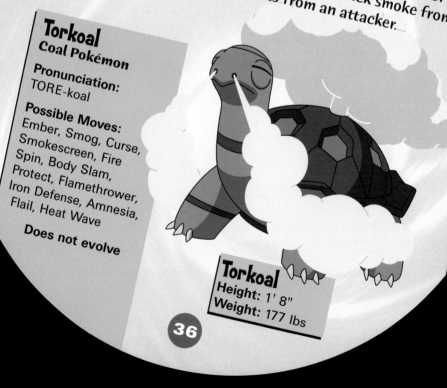

## HOENN

The source of this Pokémon's fire power is coal. To fuel up, **Torkoal** digs for coal in mountains and stores the coal in its shell. If **Torkoal** runs out of coal, it grows weaker. **Torkoal** will spout thick smoke from its nose and shell when it retreats from an attacker.

### Torkoal
Coal Pokémon

**Pronunciation:**
TORE-koal

**Possible Moves:**
Ember, Smog, Curse, Smokescreen, Fire Spin, Body Slam, Protect, Flamethrower, Iron Defense, Amnesia, Flail, Heat Wave

**Does not evolve**

### Torkoal
Height: 1' 8"
Weight: 177 lbs

36

# Hall of Fame Fire Battle: Charizard vs. Blaziken

Quick! Think of the toughest Fire Pokémon around. Did you say **Charizard?** Or did you say **Blaziken?** Both are hard to beat in battle.

Imagine how sparks would fly if these two battled each other. That's just what happened when Ash competed in the Johto League Silver Conference. It was one of the best Fire Type battles ever!

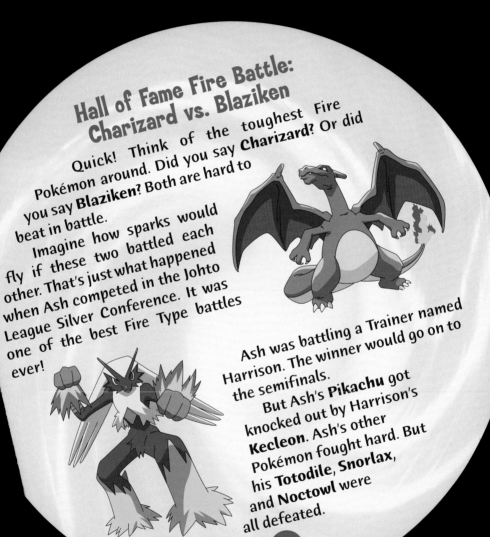

Ash was battling a Trainer named Harrison. The winner would go on to the semifinals.

But Ash's **Pikachu** got knocked out by Harrison's **Kecleon**. Ash's other Pokémon fought hard. But his **Totodile**, **Snorlax**, and **Noctowl** were all defeated.

Then Harrison used his **Houndoom** against Ash's **Bayleef**. **Houndoom**, a Fire Pokémon, had an advantage over **Bayleef**, a Grass Pokémon. But **Bayleef** used its Vine Whip attack to close **Houndoom's** mouth. **Bayleef** won!

Harrison threw out **Blaziken**, his last Pokémon. Ash was thankful he had saved his **Charizard** for last. The two mighty Pokémon battled it out in a fiery showdown.

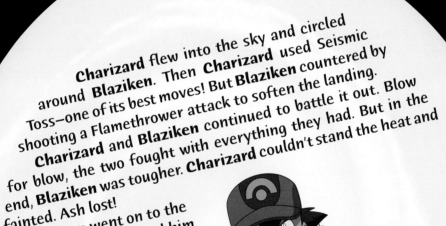

**Charizard** flew into the sky and circled around **Blaziken**. Then **Charizard** used Seismic Toss—one of its best moves! But **Blaziken** countered by shooting a Flamethrower attack to soften the landing. **Charizard** and **Blaziken** continued to battle it out. Blow for blow, the two fought with everything they had. But in the end, **Blaziken** was tougher. **Charizard** couldn't stand the heat and fainted. Ash lost!

Harrison went on to the semifinals. Ash thanked him for a great battle. It was a battle he would never forget!

39

# Hot Spots

If you love Fire Pokémon, then you should check out these Pokémon Gyms. Both are great places to see Fire Pokémon battle.

## Lavaridge Town Gym

Lavaridge Town is famous for its hot springs. These are underground pools of hot water. What better place to train Fire Pokémon?

Flannery is the Gym Leader in Lavaridge Town. She got the Gym from her grandmother. Flannery loves to use Fire Pokémon when she battles.

Ash could not wait to battle Flannery. But Team Rocket stole her **Torkoal!** Ash helped her get it back. Then they battled. Flannery used her **Magcargo**, which had just evolved from **Slugma**.

It was a good battle, but Ash beat Flannery. He won his fourth badge in the Hoenn region!

## Cinnabar Island Gym

Cinnabar Island is home to a hidden Gym inside a volcano. Ash found the Gym there and battled Blaine, the Gym Leader. Like Flannery, Blaine only used Fire Pokémon.

In the first battle, Ash could not beat Blaine's Fire Pokémon. Ash thought he lost his chance at a badge. But then Team Rocket froze the entire Gym! The volcano walls began to crack. Ash and his friends used their Pokémon to fix the cracks. Blaine let Ash battle again. This time, Ash beat Blaine. He earned a Volcano Badge!

**Tip:**
There is a store in Lavaridge Town where you can buy an item for your Fire Type Pokémon to hold called **Charcoal**. This item increases the strength of your Pokémon's Fire attacks in battle.

# Meet
# Professor Birch

Professor Birch lives in the Hoenn region. He helps Trainers start their Pokémon journeys, just like Professor Oak does in the Kanto region. We sat down and talked to Professor Birch. Here is what he had to say.

## Where is your lab?

My lab is in Little Root Town in the Hoenn Region.

## What do you do when new Trainers come to see you?

First I let them choose a Pokémon to start with. In Hoenn, they can choose **Torchic**, a Fire Pokémon; **Treecko**, a Grass Pokémon; or **Mudkip**, a Water Pokémon. Then I give them a Pokédex so that they can learn about the Pokémon they will meet on their journey.

### How do you know so much about Pokémon?

Many professors like to stay in the lab to learn about Pokémon. I like to get out in the field. I think you can learn a lot about Pokémon by watching them in the wild.

### Did anything exciting ever happen to you in the wild?

Once I got trapped by a pack of wild **Poochyena**. A Trainer named May helped me. She threw me a Poké Ball. I used my **Mudkip** to blast the **Poochyena** with water.

### Good move!

Thank you. I think every professor should know how to battle Pokémon. I have also used **Torchic**, **Treecko**, **Wailord**, and **Tropius** in battle.

### Any last word for new Pokémon Trainers?

Yes. Never give up! You will get better the more you practice.

Thank you,
Professor Birch!

# All About
## Pokémon Centers!

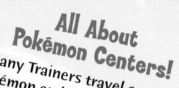

Many Trainers travel around to catch new Pokémon and earn badges in Gyms. It is a great way to become a better Trainer. But what happens when your Pokémon gets hurt, or when you need a place to sleep?

You go to a Pokémon Center, of course. You can find a Pokémon Center in just about every city. Here are some of the things you can do there:

✹ **Find Nurse Joy.** Many Pokémon Centers have a Nurse Joy. She will heal your Pokémon if they are hurt. Sometimes Nurse Joy has a Pokémon helper named **Blissey. Blissey** is a Happiness Pokémon. It loves to heal Pokémon who are sick.

✳ **Make a Call.** You can use the video phone to call home. Ash often calls the labs of Professor Oak and Professor Birch to get advice about his Pokémon.

✳ **Eat and Sleep.** Pokémon Centers help Trainers rest and gain energy between battles. You can get good food there for free. You can sleep in the Pokémon Center, too. While you're at it, you might as well get cleaned up!

✳ **Talk with Other Trainers.** At a Pokémon Center, you will meet Trainers from all over. Talk with them. They can give you tips on training your Pokémon. Of course, you might meet Trainers you don't want to talk to. Ash sometimes runs into his rival Trainer Gary Oak. Ash is never too happy about that.

## So Long!

Whew! You must be hot after reading about all of those Fire Pokémon. Maybe you should drink a big glass of water. Better yet, find a Water Pokémon to cool you off with a Water Gun move!

By now, you should be a Master in Fire Pokémon. So what are you waiting for? Go out there and catch some Fire Types! You will find that every battle with a Fire Type is filled with action and energy. And don't forget to check out www.Pokemon.com/MastersClub for more tips on caring for your Fire Pokémon. So have fun—and be careful not to get burned!